Grandfather's Gift

by Dan Secord

Illustrations by Dwight Nacaytuna

Print information available on the last page

Rev. date: 09/24/2015

To order additional copies of this book, contact:
Xlibris
1-888-795-4274
www.Xlibris.com
Orders@Xlibris.com

Dedicated to all my grandchildren.

Author Dan Secord is one of eight children, and a middle child. He grew up in a Protestant parsonage which he refers to as a glasshouse, his father being a rural pastor and minister. Born in Byron, Michigan in 1951, his family moved to the Pacific Northwest of the United States in 1958. There followed several moves from small town to small town as ministers were often transferred around his father's denominational conference according to policy. Mr. Secord left home upon graduation from High School in 1970, attending two undergraduate schools seeking his life focus and has six years of education before setting on a Bachelor of Arts in Bible and Theology from Toccoa Falls College, in Toccoa, Georgia. He then attended a graduate course in Denver, Colorado earning a Masters of Divinity in 1983. Later, he returned to a graduate program and earned a Th.D in Ministry in 2008.

Mr. Secord, works as a gentleman-laborer at a resort on the north Oregon Coast, and fulfills his heart vocation as a Chaplain in local senior care facilities representing the National Nursing Home Ministries headquartered in Portland, Oregon.

Mr. Secord has a blended family of five children and twelve grandchildren, with a thirteenth grandchild on the way.

Chapter One

Once there was a man who had three children and no wife. Life was filled with things he must do, and he was having no fun. He felt lonely without a wife. He thought, "*I must find a quiet place to puzzle out my life.*" So he traveled to the ocean and walked onto the beach. He saw the sand, the sky, and the open sea. He felt the cool breeze brushing his face. He heard the waves crashing into the surf at his feet. It seemed they whispered "peace, peace, peace". He thought, "all three, the sand, sky, and the sea work together as one." He said this is "unity." So he sat down on a grassy dune to study what he saw before him. He thought "this is just like my life, but with one piece missing." And he said to himself , "*I need unity in my life. I see I need a wife to complete my life.*"

So he remained in this settlement at the beach, enjoying the rest he'd found for more than his feet. And on the morrow he met a woman who had two children and no husband. She had a spirit like the spirit of this place by the sea. Her spirit being gentle and kind like the caressing breeze at the beach. This man and woman liked each other, and soon spend much time together. He called her " his gentle breeze" for being near her made him feel the tranquility of the sea.

Not long after, they gazed into one another eyes and said, "*We could make a blended family together.*" Haw! Yea! So they married. Then he went home, packed his things and moved with his children to the town by the Great Ocean. This is how a lonely man became the father of five children he quickly loved very much.

This blending family enjoyed a wonderful newness together. They would go to the beach for a day of sunshine and play. They would enjoy watching the waves wash in and out, dig day forts in the sand dunes, and play "Hide-and-Seek" in the tall grasses. They would build a bonfire, roast hot dogs and eat marshmallow smoors. Then as afternoon ended they watched the brilliant sunsets of golden orange, red, and purple. They saw the sun dropped down, down, down behind the horizon like it was falling in the sea. As evening came, the children would snuggles into beach blankets, and see the night sky came alive with sparkling stars. This is the time the children would say, "father tell us the story of Roger Rokk, the Badger." It was a favorite story he had created just for them. And as he began, all would be quiet as their minds imagined the story he told. Listening, they watched the embers in the fire glow melt away into darkness. Late around midnight this family of campers would trudge home happy and satisfied with all their fun that day.

BUT not all things in the new family were perfect. For the man did not have much money, nor did he have a big house where they all could live. So they moved into a small house which soon filled with many things families need. This made their home so crowded the children shared bedrooms in which to sleep. And the family lived around stacks of boxes holding items which could not be displayed. One day his kind wife said in frustration, *"Your a collector! And I am not! Why don't you get rid of some of these useless things!"* He understood her feelings about the tight quarters they all shared. But the man saw value in the boxed things he kept and knew they could be useful to the family. So he stored these extra items in his add-on garage. (And every so often one of the stored items found a place in their house again.)

Chapter Two

NOW their house sat on the north end of the settlement near the Great Ocean. The house had shake siding painted grey with white trim. And it had a large fireplace and chimney. So he put all the buoys he had found at the beach on a rope. He painted them white, then hung them on his chimney like a necklace. This matched the white trim of the windows. He thought it was a fine decoration, and many people who saw this said so too. His wife just shook her head and sighed. *"Huammm* It was not the kind of decoration she expected. But really he did it just for fun.

His wife said to herself, *"I get this picture. I can see we will have things everywhere if I do not claim some space for things I want too."* So she made flower beds all around the house growing orange nasturtiums, wild yellow iris and pretty pink carnations. The man thought this was fine indeed. So he built a sun room on the back side of their house right where the morning Sun would rise and warm the house each day. And a little at a time, space was found or created to make living a bit more comfortable and easy.

On the north end of town their house sat in the middle of seven acres of untouched nature with no neighbors. There were some tall Pine trees, a few Alders, and a scattering of Laurel bushes. Therefore the land made a great place to run and play for the kids. Plenty of space for a noise barrier from those next door. But most of all, around the house grew five acres of wild Scotch Broom, up to ten feet tall. His kids loved to run and play in this maze like a miniature forest. But to his dismay his wife said, *"I do not like that Scotch Broom, it makes my eyes water and stuffs up my nose. Please cut down those bushes!"* So he cleared the bushes back fifty yards from his house, and let the kids play further out in the maze of bushes. Soon kids all around the settlement wanted to come and play at their home. Some even asked the man and his wife if they could come and live with them in their small dwelling. The man and his wife were surprised to find many kids wanting to live at their house. But it was just too small.

One day a friend came to see the man and said, "You remember my friend John, he has worked some with us...? His house burnt down and ever since he has been sleeping under bridges for shelter in town...and I do not think this is best. You have all this maze of Scotch Broom, if I provide a tent, may he camp out there until we find another home for him?" The man knew and liked John so he said to his wife, "What do you think? May John camp in the scotch broom for a time? It is Summer and weather will be good for sometime...perhaps he will find another solid house for a home for the Winter. His wife said, "I know John and he is good man. We do not have much...but we can help him in this way. Tell him "Yes" he may stay there and we will instruct the kids not to bother him or his things. So, John came and stayed in a camp in the Scotch Broom until winter. Then he moved into a space inside the add-on garage until he was able to find an apartment in the center of town. And to this day they are all good friends.

Another time a good friend of the eldest son came back from oversea and brought a new bride. The new bride was a lovely girl and brought a lifetime pet with her: a huge Rottweiler. Having a pet makes it hard to find nice housing, and the bigger the pet, the harder it is to find a rentable house. And this young couple could not find a place to rent. It just so happened the eldest son went to college leaving his room empty. So the man and his wife opened the door to another unexpected guest for the time to find housing for the new bride. And the Rottweiler found a new home after six weeks. Years later, for the curiosity of all who wish to know, the count of guests in this house and location stands at thirty. Thirty kids and adults, who came, whether they were wandering, lost, or in search for a sanctuary in the ten years the blended family lived there.

Chapter Three

NOW this man needed to provide for his family so he went to work. Sometimes he worked as a mover, sometimes as a gardener, sometimes as a woodsman. And sometime for whatever jobs no one could be found to do. He worked hard every day to give his family food and clothes and shelter. He spent much time away from home trying to earn what money he could. He did not like being away from his family, yet he followed his own father's example to provide. So he continued to work and live in this house for many years.

The children of the man and his wife saw the things they did and each in their own way became like them. And then his children grew up and moved away to become grownups too! The man and his wife said, "*We need a place of our own. This house is too big for just the two of us.*" So the man and his wife moved to another house in a valley between cities. This new home is just the right size for them in a quiet adult village. And the man and wife were happy.

But when his children married and began to have children **he knew things must be done in a different manner.** He greatly loved each of them. And he wished he could bless them with many good things. Most of all, he wished he could bless them with a rich full life.

The man thought of his own father and said, *"I did not get to spend much time with my own father growing up because he was so busy all the time. I have only a few memories of us doing special things together. And each of my grandfathers worked so hard that they were not with us as I grew up. I, myself only did a little better spending time with my sons and daughter. I do not want my grandchildren to miss having a grandfather to share their life with as they grow up as I did. I must do something about this!"*

Soon, one after another, many grandchildren were born to the man and his wife until the number reached twelve! Nine boys and three very special girls, but was this the last of them? We will have to wait and see. And so he became a grandfather and his joy increased with every new birth. For babies are wonderful to hold and love. They make us forget about other struggles we face in the world on that day.

Chapter Four

So he thought and thought about this: "*What can I do to make sure my grandchildren have a full and good life?*" He said to himself, "*I can not think for them, and just give them the knowledge I have gained over the years; if I could, I would. For I am content and have peace with my life. And I know many choices not to make, having tried them myself.*" And then he laughed a little, thinking of all the silly things he had tried that had were mistakes or had not worked well. "*And I **can not** make their decisions for them, for this would take away their opportunities. They must develop strong wills and a resolve to become all they can be. So how do I help their future to be prosperous and good?*"

The man knew every child and grandchild must grow up using their own efforts. Grownups **can not** do it for them. They can only stand near by and watch them try. "*Maybe I can tell them how to make better choices at choice time,*" he thought. "*Maybe I can be there sometimes to help them recover from their mistakes quicker than I did!*" "*Maybe I can give them something to help them along their way!*"

The man thought about how unique and special each one of his grandchildren were wishing to give them a gift. He thought of a gift he could give them. But that would not do. He said, *"I can not give them all the same gift because they will not all need the same things to become the person they were made to be."* Children, like grownups are often very different in wants, and needs. And they express themselves in different ways because the gift of life within each one is unique.

Again the man thought about this for a long, long time. And then he knew what it was he should do. And he smiled. "Yes," that would be perfect," he said to himself. He would spend time with each one and discover what would help them the most. He said to himself, *"I will treat each one of my grandchildren special, and I will tell them to call me **Grandpa Dan**."* And this was his plan. He would **put in** his own life schedule, *time* to be with his grandchildren. He would do what they were doing. He would watch and support his grandchildren's interest. And he was sure he would find ways to help.

Chapter Five

Grandpa Dan said to his wife, *"We must make our house a place our grandchildren will like to come and visit us."* His wife said, *"Yes, we must help them grow, let us clear a space on the book shelves for some books they can read or we can read to them."* So they did just that. Then his wife said, *"Let us make this cabinet for toys for them,"* so they did. They filled a cupboard with toys for visiting grandchildren. There are little toy cars, trucks, and motorcycles in that cupboard. And stuffed animals, gadgets that light up and make tunes, action hero figurines, and Baby dolls with which to play. There are Builder Bob's that play recorded messages, toy legos and balls to roll across the floor. In another cupboard his wife put arts and craft for drawing and coloring; for she had worked in an elementary school. And Grandpa Dan brought home a miniature card table just the right size for these little ones. It has three different colored folding chairs for little ones to sit at the table. Just right for having tea parties with miniature tea sets.

Sometimes Grandpa Dan traveled to other countries and places far away. When he returned home he would bring interesting items he had found for his grandkids. These items would be placed around his front room for them to find. There were figurines of dolls, frogs, elephants, angels, flags of other nations, and old fashioned toys he brought. And lots of photographs of the places he had been.

Then Grandpa Dan also decided to create an area for his grandchildren to play in the back yard. So he built a playhouse. It was a tall playhouse built on a platform four feet up from the ground. It had windows and door ways and gangplanks to walk on outside the house. Then he built a ladder that lead up to a crows nest on the roof for spying into the distance. Next, he built a porch in front of the main doorway with a ramp way attached to the side of the raised porch for entrance.

Then he spied his large Spruce tree nearby. And he thought, *"I have a large rope I can hang on a branch for a swing."* So he climbed up into his Spruce tree and tied his rope on two branches for extra safety. Then he said, *"I need a seat for my grandkids to sit on."* So he built a seat for his swing. And Grandpa Dan was happy with what he had done. "But one thing is missing," he said. *They have no place to dig. I must make a sand box for them to play in."* And so he did. All these things he did for his grandkids who he wished to come visit and play.

Chapter Six

Soon, Grandpa Dan's sons and daughter came to visit and brought their children along. At first, the children acted shy because Grandpa's home was new to them and they did not know the rules. But soon they understood they were loved and wanted at Grandpa and Grandma's house. And they began to explore. So Grandma showed them the cabinets, cupboards and shelves just for them. They liked this very much. And they played and colored and read some books. Grandpa even showed them how to built a house with chairs and blankets in the front room. They thought this was grand. Then Grandpa said, "I have something to show you, come outside."

And outside the grandchildren squealed with delight when they saw the things prepared for them. They ran with excitement to explore the fort, the swing and sandbox. Grandpa was helping create good memories for their lives.

So one day Grandpa Dan said to Teagan May and her sister Taylynn, "Let's read a story..." And these two granddaughters ran to the bookshelves to grab their favorite story for Grandfather to read. Then they sat down together and told the stories inside the books, Grandfather reading words, and the girls telling the pictures expressed on each page. And Grandpa Dan watching these two saw how differently each one child expressed their thoughts and feelings. He could see how they looked to one another, yet had very individual ideas. It was delightful to watch, and he was pleased. The man's wife said, "Girls would you like to help me cook in the kitchen?" Away they raced to help. Standing on stools to watch what grandmother was doing, stirring with big wooden spoons, or great grandmothers egg beater was grand. They learned how to cut up vegetables, make soups, and prepare juices for the dining table.

Another day Grandpa Dan said, "Lets go for a walk..." to Teagan and Taylynn. For Grandfather lives in a park for seniors. It was quieter than in town and had pleasant and safe spaces for people to stroll about. Many seniors grow beautiful flower gardens. They like to design their homes and front yards with interesting themes. One was full of trolls, another had animals like bears and wild life, and a third painted pictures of elk, deer and people on the side of their garage. The people living here are friendly and like to chat. When it rains in the park there are night crawler worms on the roadway, and many kinds of birds fly round about overhead. Many seniors put up bird feeders to attract visitors. And there are two ponds in the park where Grandfather lives. Canadian geese, Black ducks and green-headed Mallards with their speckled female mates land every day like flying boats, to swim about on the waters.

When grandsons Anson and his brother Corbin come to visit, they too want to walk around the parkway where Grandfather lives. For these two it is feeding the wild ducks and geese that hold their interest, and playing in the fort out back. One time Grandpa gave them nails and old boards to learn to hammer. They liked this very much. Then Grandpa saw an old bag of concrete that had been left out in the rain. It was not good for posts anymore, so Grandpa decided to break it into small pieces for hauling away. Calling the boys with their hammers he told them what need to be done. Eagerly they pounded and pounded and pounded the old block of concrete into small pieces for disposal. It was indeed great fun. Sometimes they bring their bicycles, for they have learned to ride, and they like riding around the smooth roadways of Grandfather's park; for they imagine it is a race track and they liked it. They attend BMX dirt bike races.

When Ryan and Dylan come to visit, Ryan likes "Woody, the cowboy," as his favorite action figure. Then he wants grandpa to get on his hands and knees and play "ride the horse" and "chase" from one couch to the other sometimes. Ryan and his brother live in "cowboy country" in the old West of Washington state.

Yet regardless of their ages, Grandpa Dan looked for ways to relate with each of his grandchildren. He even spent a little bit of time with the babies. He would hold each one, talk to them, and make strange and different animal like sounds to hold their attention. Deep inside Grandpa Dan believes that it is important to show them he notices them too.

When Isaac comes from the "Windy City" of Chicago he likes playing bear and growls back at grandpa, and wrestles on the floor with him.

Chapter Seven

But Grandpa Dan did not just **take time** to play with his youngest grandchildren. Four of his grandkids are ten years or older. For these, *time with* means baseball, soccer, basketball, and football. It means talking to them about their developing interests. It means band concerts, parades, and school assemblies. It means listening to their stories of the day, showing interest in their hopes and dreams. It means arguing with them over tattoos, fashions of the day, and what is responsible behavior. It means supporting each one's struggles in athletic competition and relationships with classmates and friends. And standing by them when they get into trouble.

And it means Grandpa Dan tells them stories about when he was a boy. How he caught butterflies and made a collection. And how he made bows and arrows from the Maple tree. When he danced for the first time. How he chased coyotes and rabbits in the rim rocks. That he made forts in the sand dunes. Who was his first girlfriend. Where he lived and what happened to him. For in this way he shares what he faced growing up. How he overcame troubles, and had times of success. For Grandpa Dan grew up with three other brothers and fours sisters in his own family too.

Grandpa Dan told them stories of his own father when he was a boy. About the adventures of his father, making a diving suit to explore the bottom of his home town mill pond. About going cat fishing at midnight, about watermelon picking, and walking through the cemetery after dark. These things he heard from his father. Grandpa Dan knew these stories because when his father was older in life he spent time asking his dad about his life and childhood that he might know. It was part of his plan for his grandchildren to know.

Grandpa then wrote stories to tell them what he believed about life on earth and heaven. It was not how smart one is, he believed, it is that you do something with the abilities you have. So he hugged them when he saw them, and he told them he loved them, over and over and over again.

And when he was done, he realized that he was rich, very rich indeed! But his wealth was not in houses or land, but with *richness of heart*. The very richness people were made to become filled with! This was Grandfather's gift. Giving his time, energy, and love to his own that they may prosper and be happy. And Grandpa Dan believes that God is very pleased too.

Printed in the United States
By Bookmasters